Our experience

women from Somalia, Tanzania, Bangladesh and
Pakistan write about their lives

ہمارا تجربہ

Uzoefu wetu

আমাদের

Waayahayaga

Gate
HOUSE

European year of lifelong learning

Published by Gatehouse Books Ltd, Hulme Adult Education Centre, Hulme Walk, Manchester M15 5FQ

Gatehouse is grateful for continued financial support from Manchester City Council and North West Arts Board and for financial assistance towards the development of the family literacy project and production of this book from The Esmee Fairbairn Trust, The Gulbenkian Foundation, The Manchester Guardian Society Charitable Trust, The European Year of Lifelong Learning, Kellogg's, and The Halifax Building Society

Gatehouse acknowledges the additional support & skills of Princess School and The Language & Learning Support Service, Manchester, in the work of the family literacy project where this writing was generated

Illustrations, Jenny Bowers
Photographs, page 16 J Allen Cash Photolibrary; page 21 Steve McCurry, Magnum Photos; pages 37 & 60 Nick Hayes; page 51 Christine Fitzpatrick; all other photographs, Stella Fitzpatrick
Editor, Stella Fitzpatrick. Co-editor, Fatima Mumin
Translations, Jama Omer Ahmed, Fatima Mumin, Riziki Saburi, The Translation & Interpretation Service, Manchester
Printed by The Manchester Free Press, Longford Trading Estate, M32 0JT

British Library cataloguing in publication data:
A catalogue record for this book is available from The British Library
ISBN 0 906253 53 5

Gatehouse is a member of The Federation of Worker Writers & Community Publishers

Contents

We have planned the book
to make it useful
to people who don't find reading easy.
Some stories
are printed in short lines,
so you can take a break
at a point that makes sense.
The stories are told in English
and we have translated some into Somali,
Ki Swahili, Bengali and Urdu
because these are the first languages
of the writers
and they have an equal importance
with English.

Introduction

We are a group of women who grew up in Somalia, Tanzania, Bangladesh and Pakistan, countries far away from England. This is some of our first writing in English.

We have been working together for two years at Princess School, Moss Side, as one half of a family literacy project. In the other half of the project, we support and encourage our children in school. We value both parts of this project, our own personal work and shared work with our children. We would like to thank Princess Infant and Junior Schools for their interest and encouragement. We are happy to share our experience with you. We hope you like our book and that you will understand more about us through it.

Europe Abdi, Safia Abdi, Hali Hassan Eiman, Nora Elmi, Muna Jama, Shamim Khan, Fatima Mumin, Cudoon Rooble, Riziki Saburi, Kostura Ullah.

How this book was made

The writers have shared experiences and built friendship during the two years they have worked together in the Parents' Storytelling Workshop. As part of trying to speak English and to write it down, they have told stories about families, childhoods and the countries they grew up in. These have often been expressed with support from one of the teachers who works with the group, Jama Omer Ahmed. He translates and interprets between the Somali parents, and the others. Stella Fitzpatrick, the other teacher who works with the group, is an editor for Gatehouse. Through her skills, the group has produced a magazine, *Garasho*, and parents and children have made their own family books, as well as preparing this collection. For most of the writers, working to learn English is their first opportunity to learn to read and write. Seeing their emerging writing in their first language as well as English has been important. As their confidence grows, the women in the group have expanded the range of topics they write about. Jama is there when this happens, to fine-tune an interpretation or to expand a cultural point. As work on the book continued, Fatima Mumin whose English is fluent, took on an editorial role, checking some of their writing with the Somalian writers. Riziki Saburi translated her own English texts into Ki Swahili and the Translation and Information Service run by Manchester City Council has provided translations for Kostura Ullah's writing into Bengali and Shamim Khan's writing into Urdu.

Stella Fitzpatrick

About my country

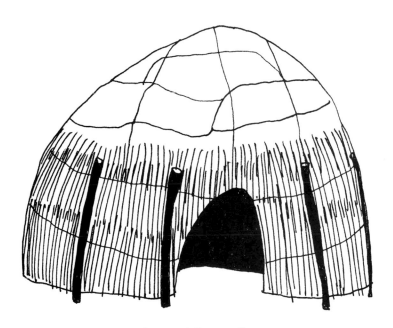

An aqal Somaali
(a traditional Somali house)

Africa

Somalia

Island
of
Zanzibar

Tanzania

Somalia

I come from Somalia.
In my country, the weather is nice.
It is not cold. It is not hot.
It is warm all the year.
We had fresh food and life was great.
I was living a happy life,
because I have two children,
and my husband was a businessman.
We lived in a large bungalow, in Hargeisa.
Then the civil war started.
Fear, shooting, fighting.
We left Somalia in 1988

Muna Jama

Tanzania and its island of Zanzibar

In Tanzania the weather is good,
about nine months is sun and hot
and three months is rainy.
Most of the people wear soft light clothes.

People who live nearest to the market
go to the market every day.
There they can buy vegetables, meat,
fish, fruits, tomatoes and other foods.

Tropical fruit & vegetables in the open market, Zanzibar city

Here is *Tanzania and its island of Zanzibar*, written in **Ki Swahili.**

Tanzania visiwani (Zanzibar)

Tanzania hali ya hewa ni nzuri.
Miezi tisa ni jua na joto
na miezi mitatu ni mvua.
Karibu watu wote huvaa nguo nyepesi.

Watu wanaoishi karibu na marikiti
wanakwenda marikiti siku zote.
Huko wananunua mboga, nyama,
samaki, matunda, tungule na vyakula vyengine.
Vyakula vyote katika nchi yangu ni freshi.

Ninakwenda dukani siku zote.
Tanzania maziwa, kuku,
nyama na siagi ni ghali,
kwa hiyo siwezi kununua vitu hivi kila siku.
Ninanunua nyama mara moja kwa wiki na
samaki kila siku
kwa sababu ni rahisi kuliko nyama au kuku.

All foods in my country are fresh.
I go shopping every day.
Milk, chicken, meat and margarine
are expensive in Tanzania,
so I cannot buy these things every day.
I buy meat once a week and fish every day
because it is cheaper than meat or chicken.

In Tanzania there are many kinds of fish
such as octopus, squid, sardine, kingfish, shark
and others. I like fried octopus
and octopus cooked with coconut
and my husband likes this too.
I cook any food with coconut.

There are many fruits and vegetables,
such as coconuts, cassavas,
many kinds of bananas, pawpaws, mangoes,
oranges, tangerines, guavas and others.
The problem of my country is
there is not enough money for daily living.
But I love my country.

Riziki Saburi

Tanzania kuna aina nyingi za samaki
kama pweza, ngisi, sadini, nguru,
papa na wengineo. Ninapenda pweza
wakukaanga
na aliyepikwa kwa nazi
na mume wangu anapenda vilevile
Ninapika kila chakula kwa nazi.
Kuna aina nyingi za matunda na mboga,
kama nazi, muhogo,
aina nyingi za ndizi, mapapai, embe,
machungwa, chenza, mapera na mengineyo.

Tatizo katika nchi yangu
hakunapesa za kutosha kwa kila siku.
Lakini ninaipenda nchi yangu.

Riziki Saburi

Bangladesh

In my country, Bangladesh,
for six months it is hot, for six months cold.
There is a big difference
between these two kinds of weather.
For only one month,
during the hot weather, in June,
it rains and rains and rains.
Maybe it stops for fifteen minutes,
then it starts again.
Lightning and thunder.
Big storm.

Kostura Ullah

Here is *Bangladesh* in Bengali

বাংলাদেশ

আমার দেশ বাংলাদেশে,
ছয় মাস গরম,
ছয় মাস ঠান্ডা।
এই দুই ধরনের আবহাওয়ার
মধ্যে বিরাট পার্থক্য।

কস্তুরা উল্লাহ

An umbrella salesman during the monsoon, in Bangladesh

Pakistan

My village in Pakistan is called Mangla.
Mangla is in Mirpur district.
There are about twenty houses in my village.
Around my village are trees, bushes and farms
with fields of crops.
On one side are hills and mountains
and, after ten minutes walk,
there are two rivers.
A little way from my village
there is a dam which makes electricity.
It is called Mangladam.

Shamim Khan

پاکستان

پاکستان میں میرے گاؤں

کا نام منگلا ہے

منگلا ڈسٹرکٹ میرپور میں ہے

میرے گاؤں میں تقریباً

بیس گھر ہیں

میرے گاؤں کے اردگرد

درخت، جھاڑیاں اور سبزیوں کے کھیت ہیں

ایک طرف چھوٹی چھوٹی پہاڑیاں اور بڑے پہاڑ ہیں

اور دس منٹ پیدل چلنے کے فاصلے پر

دو دریا ہیں

میرے گاؤں سے تھوڑے فاصلے پر

ایک ڈیم ہے

جہاں بجلی پیدا ہوتی ہے۔ اس کا نام منگلا ڈیم ہے۔

جون اور جولائی میں پاکستان میں بہت ہی گرمی ہوتی ہے۔

شمیم خان

23

A House Made Of Grass

In Somalia,
many houses are made of grass.
Somalia is hot,
and a house made of grass is cool.
We call this Somali house
the *aqal Somaali*.

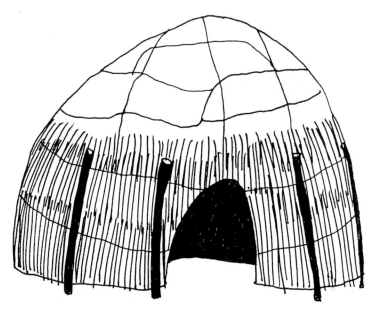

An aqal Somaali

Safia, with a grass wall made in England

My auntie weaves grass
to make the walls of the house.
She decorates as she weaves
with red, black and white wool.
She made a grass wall
in England, using English grass.
It reminds her of Somalia.

Safia Abdi.

Education in Somalia

In Somalia, the first born daughter
sometimes does not go to school.
She helps her mother at home
and learns the skills of cooking, sewing,
caring for children
and looking after plants and animals.
My mum did not go to school.
She stayed at home, as a young girl,
helping her mum.

Schools in Somalia

When children go to school in Somalia,
they are seven years old.
They stay at school until they are nineteen.
As well as state schools,
we have special religious schools
where people go for Koran lessons.
The Koran is the holy book from God.
Children go to Koran lessons
from the age of four.
Because there is a war going on in Somalia,
most of the state schools are closed now
and their buildings are destroyed.

"Why have you taken her to this school?"
My father was interested in my education.
When I was three or four years old,
my father took me to a nursery school.
I was there about two months.
My grandmother was very sorry to lose me,
and she told my mum, "She's mine.
Why have you taken her to this school?
Why didn't you ask me
before deciding to send her there?"
So my mother told my father
that my grandmother was not happy.
Next day, instead of going to nursery school,
I went to Koran lessons.
My grandmother thought this was better for me.
Later, I started school. I was the youngest.
I was six years old.

Fatima Mumin

My childhood

Because I was the only daughter,
from my childhood I have worked in the house,
sewing, cooking the food,
looking after the house.
We had a big garden
and I would plant and grow
many different plants.
I also looked after the animals,
cows, goats, chickens and hens.

Nora Elmi

It is a tradition

When a lady's husband has died,
often, the lady stays in her home.
No going out.
Family and friends help her.
For four months and ten days
she wears white colour.
Everything she wears is white,
no jewellery, no perfume.
For some of us, it is a tradition.

In Islam, Friday is a special day for all.
You wash, you go to mosque.
Everything you wear is clean.
So, on Friday, she wears a clean white dress.
She washes with another thing, not soap.
She washes with Qasil and water only.
Qasil is a plant, like henna.
You take the leaves and you dry them
then you put them in a machine
and crush the leaves to make a powder.
You mix with water and rub on your skin.
It cleans your skin better than soap.

Hali Hassan Eiman

Childbirth

In my country, Tanzania,
a mother will have her first baby in hospital.
The midwives say that the first pregnancy
is risky, so it is best to go to the hospital,

I rest one month after the birth.
My aunt and my mother-in-law
take care of me.
When I get up from bed,
I wash my baby, I put on his clothes
and breast feed the baby.
Sometimes the baby sleeps.
I like to change my baby's nappy
after every three hours.
I breast feed my baby
for three months
through the day and the night
without giving him anything to eat
except breast feeding.
Breast feeding
is better than milk powder.

Riziki Saburi

Here is *Childbirth* in Ki Swahili

Kuzaliwa kwa mtoto

Katika nchi yangu, Tanzania,
Mtoto wa mwanzo mama hujifungua spitali.
Wakunga wanasema kwamba
mimba ya kwanza
ni hatari, kwa hiyo ni vizuri kujifungulia spitali.

Ninapumzika mwezi mmoja baada
ya kujifungua.
Shangazi yangu na mkwe wangu
wananihudumia.
Ninapoinuka kutoka kitandani,
ninamkosha mtoto wangu,
ninamvisha nguo zake
na ninamnyonyesha maziwa ya kifua..
Wakati mwengine mtoto analala.
Ninapenda kumbadilisha nepi
kila baada ya masaa matatu.
Ninamnyonyesha maziwa ya kifua
kwa muda wa miezi mitatu
mchana kutwa na usiku.

Riziki Saburi

Childbirth

In Somalia.
If the mother is ill while she is pregnant,
she has her baby in the hospital,
If she's okay, she can have her baby at home.
For the first baby often, she likes to go
to the hospital.
I like to have the baby in my house,
because friends, neighbours and family
come to help.
My next baby, I will have in the hospital,
because my family is still in Somalia.

Safia Abdi

Babies get pain

You know, babies get pain,
bellyache, sometimes,
so, in Bangladesh,
my mum get this dried plant.
She add a little water
and make a drink for my son,
make him better.

Kostura Ullah

Navel String

You can tie the navel string
to whatever you choose for your child.
If you want your child to have a house,
you can bury the navel string
in the middle of the house, in the earth.
In Somalia, mostly we tie on animals
because we are nomadic people.
The offspring of that animal
from generation to generation
it belongs to the child.
If it comes to a hundred goats,
descended from that one goat,
it all belongs to the child.

Jama Omer Ahmed

Rashid

In Tanzania
when Rashid was a small baby
I take the navel string
I sent it to my grandmother.
She buried it
beside a coconut tree
and so that tree
belongs to Rashid
and the coconuts
are for Rashid.

Riziki Saburi

Mohammed

With my son Mohammed, in Somalia,
I tie the navel string
on a small goat.
I put round the neck of the goat.
Then this goat belongs to Mohammed.
When we left Hargeisa
the goat was pregnant.
We wanted to bring her
but she died.

Muna Jama

Grandparents

In Somalia, children live with their parents
until they marry.
Mostly, when a daughter marries,
she goes to her own house.
A son brings his wife to his mother's house,
or if he is rich and goes to his own house,
he takes his parents to live with him.

The grandmother bathes them

All the time,
the grandmother looks after the children.
She bathes, combs their hair, cooks for them,
looks after them.
And in the Somali tradition
children look after their parents,
any place, any time.

All her children have grown up

Sometimes, the grandmother
who is the mother's mother
takes the first born girl, at any age,
to live with her,
because all her children have grown up,
so she must have a child to help in the house.

Cudoon Rooble with Abdi Rahman & Aisha, two of her grandchildren

So, from the age of two,
I lived with my grandmother.
She came every day with me,
to my mother's house,
to care for my brothers and sisters.
She is still alive.
She's living with my mother in Somalia.
She is over ninety years old.
She's got my mother and my uncle with her.
Although she is with her children,
she likes better than that, to be with me.
When I fled to England, she was very sad.

When the civil war started
my sisters, brothers, father and myself
fled to Kenya.
But my mother stayed with my grandmother,
who did not want to leave.
We said, "Mum, there's fighting and killing,
come to Kenya."
My mother said, "How can I come?
I must stay with my mum."
And she is still there in Somalia,
looking after her mother.

Fatima Mumin

My country Somalia, in civil war.

My country in civil war, in 1988.
My son Mohammed
eight months old
and the civil war
all over the country.
In the night
my brothers died,
my friends died,
house broken,
bombs and guns.
I am frightened.
I take my son,
put him on my shoulder.
In my other hand, here, the milk.
No coat, no shoes,
nothing, only myself.
I'm frightened. Running.
I go to my mum's home.
All her children,
my sisters and brothers,
everyone ran out,
the whole family.
Walk, three, six days.

No food, no water,
no milk.
My son, Mohammed
very, very hungry.
Tired, very, very tired.
I'm coming Ethiopia from Hargeisa,
walking.
In the night
we sleep here
Oh! The enemy is here,
the gunman.
No stopping, no tired,
because you know, fright,
if you are frightened
you have energy.

At last
I'm coming Ethiopia
my father's family
and sit and rest, and water.
They have camel.

In the civil war
my father was imprisoned
when the war broke out.

Then he was let out of prison,
so he was already there, in Ethiopia.
In Ethiopia I'm sitting on the ground,
feeling calm.
No house
sleeping in the garden, outside.
I'm sleeping
I'm all right.
Insects on the ground
I don't care.

                    Muna Jama

What Makes Me Sad

I feel sad whenever I remember my family,
my father, my mother,
my relatives, my friends and my house;
how bad my country is because of the war;
the last night I was saying good-bye
to my grandmother
and remember that she was crying.

In the beginning
In the beginning of the war,
we had to leave our home in Kismayo
and travel by lorry to Mogadishu.
Mogadishu is the capital city of Somalia.
It was very difficult going from Kismayo
to Mogadishu because of the fighting.
For four months we felt safe in Mogadishu.
Then the civil war came there
and once again we started moving
from Mogadishu to Dafet.
Dafet is to the south of Mogadishu.
Soon, we had to move from Dafet to Kenya,
because the civil war had spread
to every part of Somalia.

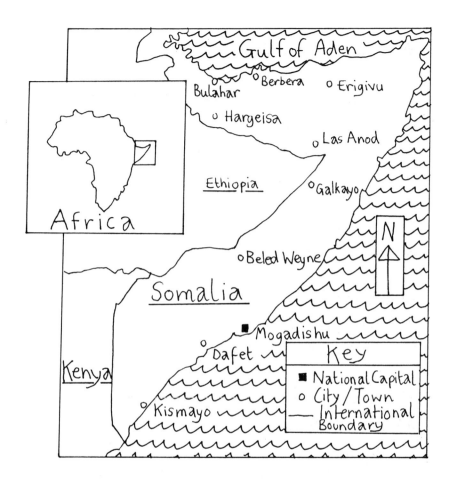

From Dafet to Kenya

The most difficult journey
was from Dafet to Kenya.
It takes fifteen days.
My husband, my mother in law,
our eight children and me
rode in the lorry with other people.
At that time I was pregnant.

43

The road was very rough and very dry.
Thirsty. No food. No safety.
Every shop was closed because of the war.
Men were in the bush.
When they hear the roaring of the truck
they would run out and aim their guns.
They take everything. Even the clothes.

At last we came to Kenya.
It's all right because it's safe.
No fighting. No fires. No danger.

Fatima Mumin

When I was young

Playing with dolls, in Somalia

We used to collect sand and old tin cans
and some leaves from trees.
We would put the sand and the leaves
into the can,
and then we would put it on three stones,
with some wood underneath,
as if we were cooking a dish.
We used the sand as the rice.
So we were cooking the rice and the sauce.
Then we would find
something that looked like a plate,
and we would serve our food.

We didn't have dolls at that time.
We used a small piece of wood.
and this was the doll.
We used to chew the top of the wood,
so it could spread out in strands.
This was the hair.
Then we found a twig or something similar
for arms and hands.
We used a piece of cloth as the dress.

Here is *Playing with dolls*, in Somali

Wiilashu waxay ciyaari jireen Xeego,
kubadda iyo Dhuumaalaysi.
Habluhu markay yar yaryihhin,
waxay soo qaadi jireen ciid.
Waxay soo qaadi jireen daasado
yar yar oo afka laga gooyey.
Waxay soo goosan jireen carmo iyo doog.
Saddex dhardhaar oo
yar yar bay samayn jireen.
Markaasay intay daasadihii
ciid iyo biyo ku shubaan,
saari jireen dhardhaarrada.
Xaabana hoosta ayey ka gelin jireen.
Daasad yaroo kale
oo ay ku jarjareen carmadii
iyo geedo ay soo gooyeen
dabka saari jireen,
waxayna ku karin jireen suugo.
Ciidda waxay ka dhigi jireen
bariiskii oo kale.
Markaasay dabeeto, intay bahalo
yar yar soo qaadaan.
ayey dabeeto ku guri jireen
oo cunto ayey ka dhigi jireen sidii
qof weyn oo dheri samaysay

We'd make a small baby
with the same material,
and say, "Here's the mum, here's her baby."
Then we would get the food
made in the tin cans
and put it down nearby, for the doll family.

The next generation were more lucky,
because they had toys, dolls and more things.

In our culture, boys and girls
don't play together, they play separately.
The only place
you can see boys and girls play together
 is in school.
 Even brothers and sisters won't play together.

Nora Elmi

48

oo cuntadii qaybinsaysa oo kale.
Markaa ka dib, caruusado
yar yar oo ah hablaho,
waxaanu ka dhigi jirney qori.
Markaasaanu korka sare intaanu
calaalino timihii oo kale ka samayn jirney.
Markaasaanu waxaanu halkan uga samayn
jirney gacmihii.
Halkaana waxaanu ugu
xidhi jirney googarad.
Halkan sarena waxaanu ugu xidhi jirney
toobkii yaraa ee shushubka lahaa.
Waxaanu u samayn jirney
barkimo yar oo lagu seexiyo iyo furaash.
Ilmihii yaraa ee ay
dhashayna hoosta ayaanu u gelin jirney.
Cuntadii iyo wixii aanu karinayna
halkanayaanu udhig dhigi jirney.

Nuuara Cilmi

49

When I was a child

When I was a child in Bangladesh,
I'm not making a doll with wood.
I'm making a doll with cloth.
My dolls were girl babies, not boys.
Girls play with girls
boys, with boys, in Bangladesh.
Me and my friend Soyzoon played
when we were small.
She came to England in 1984.
When I visited her,
she told her husband
about these small 'babies' we made,
and we laughed.

Kostura Ullah

Dipping games

In dipping games
the words matter for their sound
rather than their sense.
If you think of "Dip, dip, dip, my blue ship"
you'll see it's true.
Dipping games are played all over the world.

Dipping games from Somalia

Bille, bille,

Bille, bille,
the month is,
a meadow, desert, plain.
Cut and tie it up
with the middle one.
Turn this out!

Nora Elmi

Bil, bil,

Bil, bil,
a top, a log, a hairy old man,
a youth, and an elderly one.
Break and cut it with the tallest and middle one.
A rabbit, a squirrel, a back-firer,
a higher, a hunter, a skin-diseased one.
Get out of death!

Cudoon Rooble

Here are *Bille, bille* and *Bil, bil* in Somali, the language they started in. The English translations are opposite.

Ciyaarta bille, bille

Bille bille, bille
jire, koodaar,
ka u dheer ee dhexaad
ku jaroo ku jiqsii.
Laabo taa.

Nuura Cilmi

Bil, bil, bile jir.

Bil, bil, bile jir
Koodu, kurtimo, odey bisleh,
barbaraarta, guun guun, gumasaar, ka u dheer
ee dhexe ku jaboo ku jac sii.
Bakayle, duudle, dababukaacle, guudow,
gaadow, gobay cadhoolow, geeri bax.

Cudoon Rooble

Clapping, running game

My sister Jamila
wants to go to JigJiga.
Her father is away.
A beast appeared from Osman's farm,
The beast said, "Who shall I eat?" (runs away)

Muna Jama

And in Somali...

Walaashay Jamila

Walaashay Jamila
JigJigay raabtaayo
Aabaheed ma joogo
Beertii Cismaan na
Bahal baa ka soo baxay
Bahalkii wuxuu yidhi, "Yaan cunaa?"

Muna Jama

Song For Abdi

My son Abdi
he likes a song
that is special, for children.
Although he is growing tall,
still now, he likes to sit
on my knee, and he says,
"Please Mum,
you sing the song."
He really likes it.

After I sing it, he says,
"Sing it again."

Abdi, don't ever be without
a caring mother.
You and your brothers
live in goodness.
Don't ever be without
many brothers and sisters.
My body burns when you cry.

This is Abdi's song in Somali

Heesta Cabdi

Wiilkayga, Cabdi wuxuu jecelyahay
hees carruurta u gaar ah.
Illaa maantadan wuxuu jeclyahay
inuu jilbahayga ku fadhiisto.
Waxaanu yidhaahdaa:
"hooyo heestii ii qaad".
Runtii aad buu u jecelyahay heesta.

Markaan u qaado, wuxuu yidhaahdaa:
"hooyo iigu celi mar Kale".

Cabdiyow ha waayin hooyo ku daryeesha
Adiga iyo walaalahaa wanaagsanaadaa.
Hooyo ha waayin walaalo dhowraa.
Hooyo Markaad oydaan anna ololaa.
Cabdiyow ha waayin hooyo ku daryeesha.
Hooyo ha waayin walaalo dhowraa.

Abdi, don't ever be without
a caring mother
Don't ever be without
many brothers and sisters.
Abdi, you are a raised flag.
You and your father are excellent.
Your grandfather is good.
Your uncle is fine.

Abdi, don't ever be without
a caring mother.
Don't ever be without
many sisters and brothers.

Muna Jama

Cabdiyow calan la saarow
Hooyo, adiga iyo aabahaa
Hooyo, awowgaa wanaagsanow - waa
Hooyo, abtigaa Suubanow - waa

Cabdiyow ha waayin hooyo ku daryeesha
Hooyo ha waayin walaalo dhowraa.

Muna Jama

Song for Abdi Khalid

Abdi, Abdi, Abdi Khalid,
I pray you don't leave me
I pray you don't drag your feet.
Hobey, hobeeya.
May I read to you verses of a sacred one.
May I read to you wonderful poems.
Abdi, Abdi, Abdi,
when you are the best of all, how dare you cry?
My heart will not rest.

Europe Abdi

This is *Abdi Khalid's song* in Somali

Hobey, hobeeyaa, Cabdow

Hobey hobeeyaa.
Cabdow, Cabdow, Cabdow, waa.
Cabdow, Cabdikhaalidow waa.
Allow aanad Carari waayin
Allow aanad caqaha jiidin.
Hobeeya, hobey hobeeyaa.
War ma kuugu heesaa heesaha ma hooge.
War ma kugu geera ar galbeedshaa.
Cabdow waa. Cabdow, Cabdow, Cabdow waa.
War adoo laba dhalad dhexdoodaa.
War sideed dhayalkaa ugu ooyi
War ma kugu geeraar galbeedshaa
Hobey, hobeeyaa

Europe Abdi

Song for Hana

Hana have many prizes.
Don't be alone.
Never miss your mother,
and never be without a father.

Safia Abdi

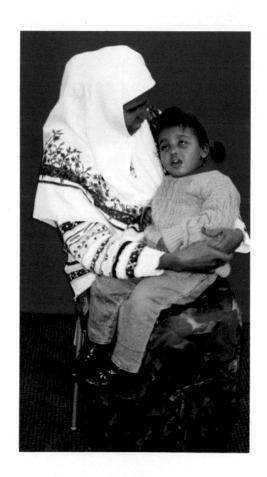

This is *Hana's song* in Somali

Heesta Hana

Hanay, hooyo hadiyad badan hel.
Weligaa ha keliyoobin.
Ha waayin hooyadaa.
Hana noqon.
Aabe La'aan.

Safia Abdi

For my children

This is a story I tell to my younger children,
to tell them to obey their parents.
"Once upon a time there was a young boy.
His name was Mohammed.
He disobeyed his mother
and walked through the forest.
Then he saw
the one who lives on grass and water
and this creature ate the boy."

Hali Hassan Eiman

Some dishes we cook

Now you know a little bit about our cultures, here are some of the dishes we cook.

Surbiyaan, from Somalia

For this meal, you need:
onion, tomato, garlic, chilli pepper, fresh
coriander, rice, lamb, tomato puree,
cardamoms, curry powder, natural yogurt,
lemon juice, cumin, saffron, butter, sultanas.

Fry the lamb in the oil.
Chop the onion, chilli pepper and tomato.
Fry them with the meat and oil.
Crush the garlic and fresh coriander.
Add cumin powder and cardamoms to this.
Put this mixture in with the lamb.
Put in tomato puree and some salt.
Put in some curry powder, and lemon juice.
Stir in some natural yogurt.

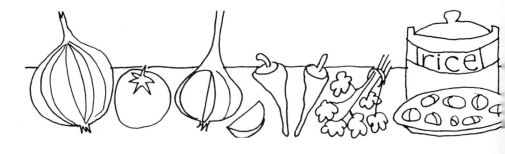

While all this is cooking, prepare the rice:
Boil some water in a pan.
Put in the rice, to cook for about 12 minutes.
Crush some cardamoms and add to the pan.
Drain the rice, when it is cooked.
Put in a little bit of butter.
Mix a pinch of saffron, with half the rice.
Leave the other half white.
Then taste the lamb mixture
and adjust the seasoning.

To serve, put the lamb mixture in a hot dish.
Put yellow rice and white rice on top of this.
Fry some chopped onion in oil,
mix it with sultanas and add some cardamom.
Put the onion and sultana mixture
on top of the rice in the serving dish.
Serve this dish hot.

Nora Elmi

Canafa, a sweet from Abu Dhabi

1

First, put water and sugar in a pan.
Let it boil and get sticky, then let it cool.
Cook some noodles and melt some butter.
Now, spread some of the butter
on the bottom of a large dish.

2

Put half of the cooked noodles on top of th
Spread cream over the noodles.
Then put sultanas on top of this.
Add the other noodles after the sultanae
and push down the mixture gently
with your hands

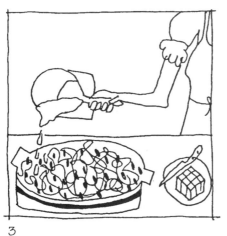

3

Pour over the rest of the melted butter.

4

Put the dish in a hot oven for 15 minute
to get brown. I use regulo 7.

Canafa, a sweet from Abu Dhabi

5

After this, take out the dish
from the oven
and turn over the Canafa
on to a plate or tray.
Put it back in the dish upside down.

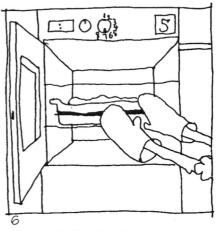

6

Now, put it back in the oven
for 5 or 6 minutes,
to brown the underside

7

Take it from the oven and pour over it
the cooled sugar and water mixture.

8

Cut it into squares.
You can eat canafa hot or cold.

Hali Hassan Eiman

Maandazi, a dish from Tanzania

1

Put some plain flour into a bowl.
Add some sugar.
Add some coconut or margarine.

2

Dissolve yeast with sugar, in warm water
and add this to the flour.

3

Mix everything in the bowl with your hand.
Then knead for 5 minutes,
until the dough is smooth.

4

When it is smooth, cut into small pieces.
Roll the pieces,
then keep them warm and covered, to rise.

Maandazi, a dish from Tanzania

5

When they have risen,
put oil into the cooking pot.
Leave the oil until it is hot.
Take some pieces of dough
and put into the hot oil.

6

Turn over after 2 minutes
and cook for another 2 minutes.

7

Then take them from the cooking pot
and the dish is ready.

Riziki Saburi

Onion Bhajis, from Bangladesh

1 - 2 onions, chopped.
1 clove fresh garlic, chopped
1 green chilli, chopped
½ cupful of plain flour
A few fresh coriander leaves, chopped
1 pinch of red chilli powder
1 pinch of garam marsala
1 - 2 eggs
1 pinch of salt
1 drop each of red colouring
and green colouring

Mix up all these ingredients.
If they are still too dry, put in a little water.
Make the mixture into small balls.
Deep fry the bhajis in oil for 10 - 15 minutes.
Test one after 10 minutes, to see if it is ready.
You can eat onion bhajis hot or cold.

Kostura Ullah

In England

My Arrival In England

When I came to England,
as soon as I came off the plane
a tall English man came to me
and he asked me what kind of passport
I am carrying with me.
I said, "A Kenyan passport."
Then he asked again,
"Are you really a Kenyan lady?" I said, "No."
He said, "So why do you carry this passport?"
I told him, "Because without documents
I can't travel."
At last, he told me not to worry
and took me to the refugee waiting room.

After a long wait,
we were vaccinated and photographed,
and we were sent
to the Refugee Arrival Project.
There also, we were waiting a long time
and they gave us a hotel to sleep in
for that first night.

A flat for me and my family

Early the next morning
a taxi took us to Camden Housing Council.
I was given a three bedroomed flat
with new beds, curtains, cupboards,
dining table and chairs and a three piece suite.

Living in London

We came at summer time. We were very lucky
because we didn't face any cold weather.
Also, my children could pick up some English
playing near my house,
in June, July and August,
before they started school.
A supermarket, schools, clinic
and a big park were near to my house.

A move to Manchester, "a dangerous city"

In London I was living in a small house
for the size of my family.
Then one day, a friend of mine
who lived in Liverpool, asked me,
"Why don't you move to Manchester?
I hope you will get a big house there
and it's a big city."

When I was preparing,
all my neighbours were sad and said,
"Oh, Manchester is a dangerous city
with gangs.
If you must move,
don't go and live in Moss Side,
because it is the worst part of Manchester".

A house in Moss Side

The first day in Manchester
when I went to ask about a house,
they told me that they have
a big house for me, in Moss Side.
I was disappointed when I heard this.
I asked if I could get a house in another area
but they told me, Moss Side is the only place
I can get a house big enough for my family.
I agreed, but I was not feeling happy.

I like Moss Side

Now, I have lived in Moss Side since 1994.
You can't imagine how much I like Moss Side
and also how quiet Moss Side is.

So, because of all these things
me and my family we feel very, very happy.

Fatima Mumin

Coming to England

I came to England in May 1995.
I arrived through Manchester Airport.
When I reached the airport, I was very scared
because I didn't know how to speak English.
I had a problem to fill in the landing card
that I was given in the plane.
But the Immigration Officer helped me to do it.
The officer asked me several questions
about my coming to England.
I told her I don't understand or speak English.
I had to show her my passport,
a letter from my husband's course,
the name of my husband,
his address and telephone number.
My husband sent me all this information
before I came.
Then she called my husband
who was waiting for me
and they spoke on the telephone.
Finally, she stamped my passport
and allowed me to go.

Riziki Saburi

In Ethiopia

I travelled from England
to see my family in Ethiopia.
I went to five places in Ethiopia
and it is very, very beautiful.
Trees with much fruit.
The weather is always good,
I drank two cups of fresh milk from a camel,
every day. It is very, very nice.
Also, meat from a camel is good.
I ate it six times during my visit.
I saw my grandmother in Ethiopia.
She's tired. She's very old.

London

I came into immigration, in London.
I had a big interview.
Before the interview, I say,
"I can't speak English very well."
He say, "You can understand English. Try."
I tried. I became very frightened
that they might send me back.
I started talking, talking, talking.
I didn't realise I knew this many words.

Muna Jama

My Name Is Europe

My name is Europe.
I have three children.
The eldest one is twelve years old.
The second child is eleven years old.
The youngest child is five years old.

My children go to school.
They are happy.
They like school.
They are learning very well.
But after that,
me and my children are worrying
because my children did not see their father
for five years.
They are missing their father.
He sends letters to them
and he telephones,
but they ask for their father, every day.

I am not happy for the last three years.

Europe Abdi

About the writers

Nora Elmi

From an early age
until now
I have been working
to bring up my children.
I have fourteen children.
I had twenty children
I lost six through miscarriage.
Now I am very tired
I am ready for a rest.

Cudoon Rooble

I was born in Kismayo,
in the south of Somalia.
When I was a young girl,
I helped my family.
I looked after the animals.
I helped my mum to build and look after
the *aqal Somaali* (family house).
When I was fourteen, I got married.
I had seven children,
but five died.
Now, I live with my son and his family.

Fatima Mumin

I was always liking to learn something.
After my secondary school,
I went to teachers' training college,
but I am sorry I didn't finish my course.
From that time till now I was trying to learn.
I have got a big family,
my husband, nine children, my cousin
and my mother-in-law.

Hali Hassan Eiman

I have nine children.
My biggest son is in Ethiopia.
My family is good.
My children are clever.
I like children.

Muna Jama

I have been in England for five years.
My children are happy and I am happy.
My children's teachers are good
because they care
and help my children at school.
I attend the parent's storytelling project
on Wednesday mornings each week.
Here, I meet with my friends,
and I work with my children.
I like learning English ,
and I am doing well.

Europe Abdi

I have lots of family.
My mother is dead
and my father also is dead
but I have lots of brothers and sisters.
I have ten sisters
I have six brothers
My sisters and my brothers
they have lots of children.
One of my sisters
she has nine children.

Kostura Ullah

I am from Bangladesh.
I have five children.
I have four boys and one girl.
My children were born
in England and Bangladesh.
I am happy to be a mother.

Riziki Saburi

I was born in 1971,
on a small island
called Zanzibar-Tanzania,
off the coast of East Africa.
 I am married with two children.
The first-born is called Rashid
and the second-born is called Abdu.
I came to Manchester to visit my husband
in May 1995.
He was on a course in Manchester.
My aim is to be able to speak English
with other people of Manchester.

Safia Abdi

I was born in Hargeisa, Somalia.
I have four sisters.
I also have six children,
two boys, and four girls.
My husband helps me with our children
because they are young.

Shamim Khan

I was born in Pakistan.
I have lived in Manchester
for eight years.
I have five children.
My children are happy
and my husband is good.

Gatehouse Books

Gatehouse is a unique publisher
Our writers are adults who are developing their basic
reading and writing skills. Their ideas and experiences
make fascinating material for any reader, but are
particularly relevant for adults working on their reading
and writing skills. The writing strikes a chord, a shared
experience of struggling against many odds.

The format of our books is clear and uncluttered. The
language is familiar and the text is often line-broken,
so that each line ends at a natural pause.

Gatehouse books are both popular and respected
within Adult Basic Education throughout the English
speaking world.They are also a valuable resource
within secondary schools, Social Services and within
the Prison Education Service and Probation Services.

Booklist available
Gatehouse Books
Hulme Adult Education Centre
Hulme Walk
Manchester
M15 5FQ
Tel: 0161 226 7152
Fax: 0161 226 8854

The Gatehouse Publishing Charity Ltd is a registered charity, no. 1011042
Gatehouse Books Ltd is a company limited by guarantee, reg no. 2619614